300-Calorie Dinner:

30 Days of Healthy, Hassle-Free Recipes

SIMPLY SVELTE

HEALTHY EATING MADE EASY

ISBN-13: 978-0988354753

FIRST THINGS FIRST

Consult with your physician before beginning
any diet and/or exercise program.

CONTENTS

ABOUT THE RECIPES

The recipes in this cookbook are designed to serve one person—you. When you make any one of these meals for yourself, you visually gauge exactly how much food amounts to 300 calories. You quickly learn the value of portion control in reaching and maintaining your ideal weight. However, if you wish to share these delicious meals with your family, any of these recipes may be doubled, tripled, or quadrupled for additional servings. Bon appetit!

Asian Chicken Stir-Fry

Olive oil cooking spray
4 oz chicken breast, cut into cubes
½ cup diced carrots
½ cup diced onion
1 tsp soy sauce
½ tsp rice vinegar
½ tsp sesame seeds
¼ tsp grated fresh ginger
2 cups broccoli florets

Lightly spritz a saucepan or wok with the olive oil cooking spray. Heat the pan over high heat. Add the cubed chicken and shake to sauté. Once chicken begins to brown, add the other ingredients. Gently stir and shake the pan to brown the vegetables. Serve immediately.

Serves 1

Calories per serving: 307

BAKED PORK CHOPS WITH APPLES

Olive oil cooking spray
4 oz center-cut pork chop, fat trimmed
1 medium apple, peeled, cored, and thinly sliced
¼ tsp nutmeg
Salt and pepper to taste

Preheat the oven to 350 degrees. Lightly spritz a small baking dish with the olive oil cooking spray. Add the pork chop, and season with salt, pepper, and nutmeg. Arrange the apple slices on top. Lightly cover the dish with aluminum foil and cook until pork is cooked through, approximately 40 minutes. Serve immediately.

Serves 1
Calories per serving: 260

Serve with 1 cup steamed kale (seasoned with salt and red pepper flakes, if desired) for a 296-calorie meal.

Barbecue Chicken and Potato Casserole

3 oz boneless chicken breast, cut into large cubes
1 potato, cut into large cubes
1 Tbsp barbecue sauce
1 Tbsp fresh rosemary

Preheat oven to 375 degrees. Combine all ingredients in a baking dish. Bake for 1 hour or until chicken has reached desired doneness.

Serves 1
Calories per serving: 323

Beef Stew with Mushrooms

3 oz beef stew meat
1 Tbsp tomato paste
1 clove garlic, minced
8 pearl onions
8 oz assorted wild mushrooms
1 medium carrot, cut into rounds
1 oz red wine
2 Tbsp beef broth, boxed or canned
1 tsp fresh thyme
1 tsp fresh parsley
Salt and pepper to taste

Preheat oven to 325 degrees. Combine all ingredients in a baking dish. Bake for 1 hour or until stew meat has reached desired doneness.

Serves 1
Calories per serving: 325

Black Bean and Corn Soup

Olive oil cooking spray
1 Tbsp minced onion
1 Tbsp minced bell pepper (sweet or spicy variety, to taste)
1 cup canned black beans, with juice
1 cup canned corn
1 fresh tomato, chopped
1 cup chicken broth, boxed or canned

Lightly spritz a small soup pot with one spray of olive oil cooking spray. Place the soup pot over medium heat on the stove. Add the onion and pepper, and brown until soft. Add the black beans, corn, and tomato, and stir to incorporate. Add the chicken broth. Turn the heat to low and simmer for 30 minutes. If desired, garnish with fresh chopped green onion or cilantro.

Serves 1
Calories per serving: 296

Cheesy Beef and Broccoli Casserole

3 oz ground beef (95% fat-free), browned and drained
1 cup broccoli florets, chopped into 1-inch pieces
½ cup brown rice, cooked
2 oz fat-free cheddar cheese

Preheat oven to 350 degrees. Combine all ingredients in a baking dish. Bake for 30 minutes, or until cheese is bubbly.

Serves 1
Calories per serving: 347

CHICKEN PICCATA

Olive oil cooking spray
1 Tbsp whole wheat flour
3 oz boneless chicken breast
1 lemon
1 Tbsp fresh parsley
Salt and pepper to taste

Lightly spritz a small skillet with one spray olive oil cooking spray. Place the skillet over medium heat on the stove. Lightly coat the chicken breast in flour, and shake off the excess. Brown chicken breast evenly on each side. Squeeze the juice of 1 lemon over the top, and reduce heat to low. When chicken is cooked through, add the fresh parsley, salt and pepper. Serve immediately.

Serves 1
Calories per serving: 334

CITRUS CHICKEN

Olive oil cooking spray
4 oz bone-in chicken breast
½ cup orange juice
½ tsp mustard
1 cup green bell peppers, chopped
1 small orange, peeled and chopped
Salt and pepper to taste

Preheat the oven to 375 degrees. Combine ingredients in a small roasting pan. Cook until chicken is cooked through, approximately 40 minutes.

Serves 1
Calories per serving: 269

Serve with 2 cups spinach dressed with 1 tsp olive oil and ½ tsp vinegar to create a 322-calorie meal.

COMFORT PASTA

¾ cup dry whole wheat penne
¼ cup fat-free ricotta cheese
3 oz marinara sauce from a jar

Cook penne until al dente. While the pasta is cooking, combine the marinara sauce and ricotta cheese in a bowl, and mix well. Drain the pasta, and add the sauce to the hot pot to warm it. Add the pasta back to the pot and mix well to coat the pasta. Serve immediately.

Serves 1
Calories per serving: 324

COQ AU VIN

4 oz bone-in chicken breast
1 Tbsp diced shallots
1 carrot, diced
1 Tbsp chicken broth, boxed or canned
1 tsp red wine
1 tsp tomato paste
10 mushrooms, sliced
1 Tbsp fresh parsley, chopped
1 tsp fresh thyme
1 bay leaf

Preheat oven to 375 degrees. Combine all ingredients in a roasting pan, and roast until chicken is cooked through and dish is bubbly, approximately 60 minutes.

Serves 1
Calories per serving: 235

Serve with 2 cups mixed greens dressed with 1 tsp olive oil and ½ tsp vinegar to create a 288-calorie meal.

Country Fried Steak

3-oz piece of cube steak
1 Tbsp whole wheat flour
1 tsp fresh rosemary
Salt and pepper to taste
Olive oil cooking spray

Pound cube steak flat. Season with flour, rosemary, and salt and pepper. Lightly spritz a small skillet with olive oil cooking spray. Place skillet over medium heat on the stove. Brown the cube steak on each side. Add a little water if it begins to stick.

Serves 1
Calories per serving: 170

Serve with 1 cup black-eyed peas and 2 cups collard greens to create a 285-calorie meal.

Creamy Beef Goulash

Olive oil cooking spray
½ cup onion, diced
½ cup bell green bell pepper, diced
3 oz lean ground beef
1 oz can tomatoes
¼ cup beef broth
1 Tbsp fat-free sour cream
½ cup cooked whole wheat noodles

Lightly spritz a small skillet with one spray of olive oil cooking spray. Place the skillet over medium heat on the stove. Brown the onion and green pepper until soft. Add the ground beef and brown until cooked through. Add the tomatoes and beef broth, and lower heat to a simmer for 5 minutes. Turn off the heat and stir in the sour cream, mixing well. Serve over cooked whole wheat noodles.

Serves 1
Calories per serving: 242

Serve with 2 cups mixed greens dressed with 1 tsp olive oil and ½ tsp vinegar to create a 295-calorie meal.

DRUNKEN CHICKEN

4 oz boneless chicken breast
1 oz tomato paste
1 fl oz beer
½ tsp paprika
Salt and pepper to taste

Preheat oven to 350 degrees. Combine all ingredients in a baking dish. Bake for 40 minutes.

Serves 1
Calories per serving: 255

Serve with ¼ cup brown rice and 1 cup green beans to create a 295-calorie meal.

HOME-STYLE PORK CHOPS

Olive oil cooking spray
4 oz center-cut pork chop, fat trimmed
1 Tbsp tomato paste
1/2 tsp brown sugar
1 tsp vinegar
Salt and pepper to taste
½ cup Vidalia onion, chopped
1 cup green bell pepper, chopped

Lightly spritz a small saucepan with olive oil cooking spray. Place on the stove over medium heat. In a small mixing bowl, add the tomato paste, brown sugar, vinegar, salt and pepper, and whisk together. Lightly brown the pork chop on each side in the hot pan. Add the onion and bell pepper and brown until soft. Slowly pour the sauce over the top, and allow to simmer one minute.

Serves 1
Calories per serving: 234

Serve with ½ of a medium baked potato and 1 small pat of butter to create a 302-calorie meal.

Italian Pot Roast

3-oz portion of boneless beef roast, with fat trimmed
1 tsp Italian seasoning
1 clove garlic, mashed
¼ cup chopped sundried tomatoes
¼ cup kalamata olives
¼ cup beef broth, boxed or canned
¼ cup pearl onions

Preheat oven to 325 degrees. Combine all ingredients in a baking dish. Bake for 1 hour or until roast has reached desired doneness.

Serves 1
Calories per serving: 300

Lebanese Meatballs

Olive oil cooking spray
3 oz ground turkey, 97% fat-free
½ tsp cinnamon
1 tsp cumin
1 Tbsp flat-leaf parsley, coarsely chopped
Salt and pepper to taste
1 Tbsp tomato paste
1/4 cup cooked brown rice
1 oz whole wheat spaghetti, broken into small pieces and cooked

In a mixing bowl, combine the turkey, cinnamon, cumin, parsley, and salt and pepper. With your hands, form small, gumball-sized meatballs. Lightly spritz a small skillet with one spray of olive oil cooking spray. Place the skillet over medium heat on the stove. Carefully place the meatballs in the skillet and shake to brown on all sides. While the meatballs are cooking, place the tomato paste in a bowl and thin with water until it is liquid in consistency. Pour tomato liquid over the meatballs and turn heat to low. Simmer for one minute. Combine the rice and pasta, and pour the meatball mixture over the top.

Serves 1
Calories per serving: 317

Serve with 2 cups fresh spinach dressed with lemon, olive oil and vinegar to create a 294-calorie meal.

LENTIL SOUP

Olive oil cooking spray
¼ cup diced onion
1 stalk celery, diced
1 carrot, diced
4 leaves fresh spinach, chopped
1 2-oz slice of ham, diced
½ cup dried lentils
1 cup chicken broth, boxed or canned
1 oz canned chick peas, drained
½ tsp cumin
1 wedge of lemon

Lightly spritz a small soup pot with one spray of olive oil cooking spray. Place the soup pot over medium heat on the stove. Add the onion, carrot, and celery, and brown until soft. Add the spinach, ham, and lentils, and stir until spinach leaves are wilted. Add the chicken broth and chick peas. Bring to a boil. Add the cumin. Turn the heat to low and simmer for 1 hour. Squeeze lemon juice into the soup and stir.

Serves 1
Calories per serving: 241

Moroccan Chicken

1 bone-in chicken thigh
½ cup butternut squash, cut into chunks
10 strips red bell pepper
1 oz tomato salsa
1 oz canned diced tomatoes
1 Tbsp raisins
¼ tsp cumin
¼ tsp cinnamon
1 Tbsp canned chick peas, drained
1 tsp fresh flat-leaf parsley, coarsely chopped

Place all ingredients in a slow cooker and cook for 8 hours on low heat.

NOTE: Recipe may be doubled, tripled or quadrupled for additional servings.

Serves 1
Calories per serving: 242

Serve with 1 small whole wheat flatbread to create a 312-calorie meal.

Pasta Fagioli

Olive oil cooking spray
1 slice Canadian bacon, diced
1 tsp fresh rosemary
1 oz tomato paste
½ cup canned white kidney beans, drained
¾ cup whole wheat elbow noodles, cooked
1 Tbsp grated Parmigiano-Reggiano cheese

Lightly spritz a small skillet with one spray of olive oil cooking spray. Place the skillet over medium heat on the stove. Brown Canadian bacon and rosemary. Add the tomato paste and kidney beans. Add the noodles, and mix well. Sprinkle grated Parmigiano-Reggiano cheese on top upon serving.

Serves 1
Calories per serving: 303

Pasta with Lemon and Parsley

Olive oil cooking spray
1 cup fresh tomato, chopped
½ tsp grated lemon rind
½ cup fresh basil, chopped
½ cup fresh flat-leaf parsley, chopped
¾ cup (2 oz) whole wheat penne, cooked

Lightly spritz a small skillet with one spray of olive oil cooking spray. Place the skillet over medium heat on the stove. Add the tomatoes and lemon rind, and sauté for one minute. Add the herbs. Serve over whole wheat penne, with grated Parmigiano-Reggiano cheese on top.

Serves 1
Calories per serving: 180

Serve with 12 large grilled shrimp to create a 292-calorie meal.

Peas and Rice

Olive oil cooking spray
½ cup minced onion
1/2 cup brown rice
1 cup frozen green peas
1 cup chicken broth
1 Tbsp Parmigiano-Reggiano cheese

Lightly spritz a small skillet with one spray of olive oil cooking spray. Place the skillet over medium heat on the stove. Add the onion, and sauté for one minute. Add the remaining ingredients and allow to simmer until rice is al dente. Serve with grated Parmigiano-Reggiano cheese on top.

Serves 1
Calories per serving: 352

SALMON WITH FRESH HERBS

1 4-oz salmon filet
1 tsp olive oil
1 tsp lemon juice
½ tsp fresh chives
1 tsp fresh chopped parsley
1 tsp fresh chopped basil
Salt and pepper to taste

Preheat the oven to 375 degrees. In a small baking dish, place the salmon filet, and add the additional ingredients. Bake until salmon is cooked to desired doneness, approximately 20 minutes.

Serves 1
Calories per serving: 296

Savory Sausage

1 4-oz lean chicken sausage
1/4 cup brown sugar
1 Tbsp spicy brown mustard

Preheat the grill. In a small mixing bowl, whisk the sugar and mustard into a glaze. Grill the sausage. During the last 2 minutes of grilling time, brush the glaze on the sausage, and turn to coat evenly.

Serves 1
Calories per serving: 196

Serve with 2 cups fresh arugula dressed with lemon, olive oil and vinegar to create a 294-calorie meal.

SOUTHERN-STYLE MINESTRONE

Olive oil cooking spray
¼ cup diced onion
1 stalk celery, diced
1 carrot, diced
4 leaves fresh spinach, chopped
½ cup okra (fresh, frozen or canned)
1 oz canned black-eyed peas, drained
1 medium tomato, chopped
1 cup chicken broth, boxed or canned
1 oz cooked chicken meat, shredded
¼ cup cooked brown rice
Rind of a block of Parmigiano-Reggiano cheese

Lightly spritz a small soup pot with one spray of olive oil cooking spray. Place the pot over medium heat on the stove. Saute the onion, celery, and carrot until soft. Add the spinach, okra, corn, and black-eyed peas. Saute for one minute. Add the tomato. Add the chicken broth and the Parmigiano-Reggiano cheese rind. Bring to a boil. Let cook for 30 minutes. Add the chicken meat and brown rice just before serving.

NOTE: Recipe may be doubled, tripled, or quadrupled for additional servings.

Serves 1
Calories per serving: 240

Serve with 2 cups mixed greens dressed with 1 tsp olive oil and ½ tsp vinegar to create a 314-calorie meal.

Spaghetti with Clam Sauce

1 tsp olive oil
1 clove garlic, peeled
1 cup whole wheat spaghetti, cooked
2 oz canned chopped clams, with juice
1 Tbsp fresh flat-leaf parsley
½ lemon, cut into wedges

Heat olive oil in a skillet over medium heat. Add the peeled garlic clove, and stir it in to flavor the oil. Before it browns, remove the garlic clove and dispose. Add the clams with their juice. Add the parsley. Turn off the heat. Pour the drained, cooked spaghetti into the sauce, and use tongs to coat the noodles evenly.

Serves 1
Calories per serving: 303

SPICY ROAST BEEF SLIDERS

1 tsp olive oil
½ tsp horseradish
½ tsp dried oregano
Salt and pepper to taste
2 oz lean roast beef
1 cup fresh arugula
2 slices fresh tomato
1 whole wheat bun

In a small mixing bowl, whisk together the olive oil, horseradish, oregano, salt and pepper. Add the roast beef, arugula and tomato, and mix well to coat the surfaces with the dressing. Transfer to a whole wheat bun and enjoy.

Serves 1
Calories per serving: 326

Stuffed Acorn Squash

½ acorn squash (one whole acorn squash seeded and halved)
2 oz ground turkey (97% fat-free), browned
15 mushrooms, diced
½ cup brown rice, cooked
½ cup diced red peppers
¼ cup celery, diced
¼ cup onion, diced
½ cup chicken broth, boxed or canned

Preheat oven to 350 degrees. Place acorn squash half on a baking sheet and bake for 30 minutes. In the meantime, combine the cooked turkey and remaining ingredients in a mixing bowl. When the squash is soft, remove from the oven. Scoop out the squash flesh, and add it to the turkey mixture. Mix well. Then, turn the mixture back into the bowl-shaped rind of the squash. Bake for another 30 minutes.

Serves 1
Calories per serving: 319

TUNA CASSEROLE

3/4 cup whole wheat elbow noodles, cooked and drained
Salt and pepper to taste
¼ cup diced onion
3 oz fat-free sour cream
4 oz canned tuna, drained
½ cup shredded fat-free cheddar cheese
1/2 cup frozen peas

Preheat oven to 375 degrees. Combine all ingredients in a small baking dish. Cook approximately 1 hour, or until dish is bubbly and cheese is browned.

Serves 1
Calories per serving: 306

Veal Cutlet Dinner

2 tsp olive oil
3 oz veal cutlet, pounded flat
¼ cup whole wheat bread crumbs
2 cups fresh arugula
1 whole tomato, diced
3 lemon wedges
1 tsp grated Parmigiano-Reggiano cheese
½ tsp balsamic vinegar
Salt and pepper to taste

Heat 1 tsp of the olive oil in a skillet over medium heat. Lightly coat the veal cutlet with the bread crumbs, and shake off excess. Brown cutlet on both sides in the skillet. Place the browned cutlet on a serving plate, and top with arugula, tomato, cheese, and lemon. Season with the remaining teaspoon olive oil, vinegar, salt and pepper to taste.

Serves 1
Calories per serving: 291

VEGETARIAN ROTINI

1 tsp olive oil
1 cup chopped zucchini
1 cup cherry tomatoes, halved
1 cup yellow bell peppers, chopped
½ cup diced onion
1 tsp fresh oregano, diced
3/4 cup dry whole wheat rotini pasta, cooked al dente and drained
1 Tbsp Parmigiano-Reggiano cheese
Salt and pepper to taste

Heat the olive oil in a skillet over medium heat. Brown the vegetables in the skillet. Add the oregano. Add the cooked pasta to the pan, and gently shake to incorporate the vegetables. Add Parmigiano-Reggiano cheese, salt and pepper to taste.

Serves 1
Calories per serving: 320

ABOUT SIMPLY SVELTE

For years we've been led to believe that exercising is the key to losing weight. The truth is that reaching your ideal weight is 95% eating habits--both the quality and quantity of food that goes in your mouth consistently, each and every day. When you eat clean, track your calories, and make consistent, healthy choices, your weight stays stable--naturally! The Simply Svelte program is not a diet, and is not a fad. It's a sensible way of eating that you'll be able to stick with for life.

Connect with us online at Facebook (Simply Svelte) and Twitter (@SimplySvelte).

OTHER BOOKS BY SIMPLY SVELTE

If you enjoyed this book, check out other recipe and meal planning tools from Simply Svelte. The Simply Svelte team has put together 30 days' worth of healthy, easy-to-prepare breakfasts, lunches, and dinners that will help you lose weight and feel satisfied all day long. With minimal planning, you're on your way to simple, tasty options from Cheese Grits Casserole to Homemade Pizza and Italian Pot Roast. Mix and match the easy, delicious 300-calorie meals in these cookbooks, and you'll be amazed how you look and feel 30 days from today!

Find these books at amazon.com:

Simply Svelte's 30 Days to Thin: An Easy, 300-Calorie Mix-and-Match Plan to Keep You Slim for Life

300-Calorie Breakfast: 30 Days of Healthy, Hassle-Free Recipes

300-Calorie Lunch: 30 Days of Healthy, Hassle-Free Recipes

300-Calorie Dinner: 30 Days of Healthy, Hassle-Free Recipes

Printed in Dunstable, United Kingdom

79029737R00030